The Jesus Tree

Story by Carey Thomas Illustrations by **Katie Kelly**

The Jesus Tree

© Carey Thomas 2013

Illustrations by Katie Kelly

Published by
Meatloaf Media LLC
32 Zwicks Farm Rd
Plantsville, CT 06479

www.meatloafmedia.com

For Belle, Maci, Reuben and Grandmother Thomas

It was a crisp December morning in Coney Village. The trees were ornamented with dangling pine cones and snow had decorated the boughs like tinsel. Mackenzie and Ben peered out their frosty window at the winter wonderland. Ben could hardly wait to try his new sled and the wintry weather put Mackenzie in the mood for a little Christmas shopping.

"You are going to help Mrs. Daniels decorate her Christmas tree today," Mom announced.

Ben could hardly believe his ears. "You mean the old lady down the street?" he whined. Everyone in the neighborhood talked about Mrs. Daniels' messy yard, overgrown flower beds and the fact that she hardly ever left her house or had any visitors.

"Yes, Ben. She's getting older and can't do all of the things that she used to do. I thought it would be nice for you to help with her tree and spread some Christmas love."

Mackenzie scrunched her nose in protest. "Christmas love? Well, I would love to go shopping with my friends instead. I don't want to work all day for a grumpy old lady that I don't even know."

It was no use trying to change Mom and Dad's decision. Dad had already picked up a fresh-cut tree at Piney's Farm and before they knew it they were off to spread a little Christmas love.

Mrs. Daniels greeted them at the door with a bright toothy smile, as the aroma of fresh baked sugar cookies wafted into the chilly air. "Ooh, that tree is real pretty! Now, you come in here my friends!" she exclaimed. Mrs. Daniels was not at all grumpy. She was cheerful and rosy and her tiny cottage was cozy and neat.

Dad stuffed the tree through the little door, knocking pine needles onto the carpet. "You should really consider an artificial tree Ma'am," Dad said smiling.

Mrs. Daniels smiled back. "Nonsense! I must have a live tree. You see, it's part of my Christmas tradition. This living tree reminds me that Jesus is alive and flourishing." Mrs. Daniels looked at Dad, "Now don't you have some shopping to do? Ben and Mackenzie can stay here and help me decorate while you go and get a few things done. Now you kids go to the attic and get the decorations. Hurry!"

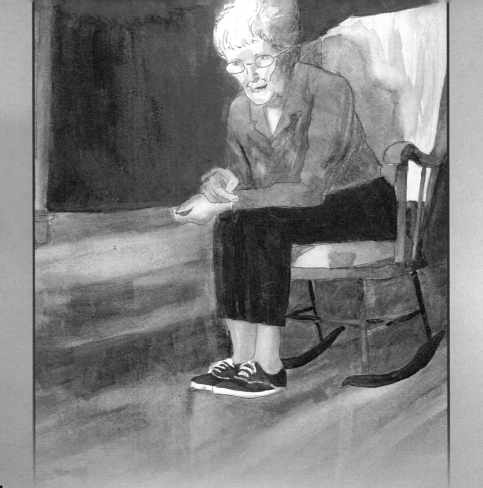

"These lights are all tangled," Mackenzie sighed as she lifted bundles of Christmas lights from the dusty boxes.

"Then I guess you better get to untangling them," laughed Mrs. Daniels.

Mackenzie rolled her eyes. She wished she could be shopping and sipping hot cocoa at the mall with her friends, but instead she had to untangle lights. The wires were a faded green color and some of the bulbs were broken or missing. "Mrs. Daniels, these lights are really old-fashioned. They sell better ones now that blink to the beat of music. Don't you think it's time for some new ones?"

"Honey, these lights are just fine. It makes no difference to me if they're old or new because they remind me that Jesus is the *light* of the world. My Bible tells me that whoever follows Jesus will never walk in darkness, but will have the light of life."

Mackenzie felt a little silly. "I never thought about Christmas lights like that before," she said. She had been so excited about Christmas, but had given very little thought to Jesus. She wove the lights carefully over one branch and under the next. As she worked she noticed that the old lights had a pretty sparkle she hadn't seen before.

Ben was busy hanging deep purple glass balls on the tree.

"Purple is the color that kings and queens wear," Mrs. Daniels piped up from her chair. "Those ornaments help me remember that Jesus is *my King*. Sometimes Jesus is called the *Prince* of Peace." The old lady paused for a moment. "You know, every decoration that goes on my tree reminds me of Jesus in some way."

"That's funny," giggled Ben. "I didn't know that the Christmas tree is supposed to be about Jesus. I thought it was just a decoration."

"It's a party decoration for Jesus' Birthday," the old woman chimed. "Still somehow, in all the activities of the season we forget about the Birthday Boy. This tree will remind me of God's love every time I look at it. I call it my Jesus Tree."

Mackenzie and Ben listened closely now as Mrs. Daniels told them more about her Jesus Tree. The gentle lady pointed to another box of decorations. Mackenzie began rummaging through it. She gasped as she lifted up a delicate hand-made angel ornament. "This is so pretty!"

"That one reminds me of the angel that appeared to the shepherds, announcing Jesus' birth. The angel told them, 'Today in the city of David a Savior has been born to you; he is Christ the Lord.'"

"These candy canes look like a shepherd's staff!" Ben said.

"That's exactly what they mean, Ben. Jesus is our Good Shepherd and He cares so much for us."

"You try the garland. See if you can guess what it means." Mackenzie studied it for a while, but she couldn't figure it out. "Why don't you hold it?" Mrs. Daniels said. Mackenzie took the shiny rope in her hands. She closed her eyes and thought about Jesus.

"I've got it!" she said. "Maybe it is like the crown of thorns that Jesus wore when He died."

"Yes, yes, yes!" Mrs. Daniels shouted excitedly, hopping up and down and clapping her hands. "Now you are getting it! We are almost done."

Mackenzie and Ben began hanging red ornaments on the tree.

"Those ones make me think of Jesus' blood that washes sins away, "Mrs. Daniels explained. "If Jesus didn't die on the cross for us, we could never be forgiven for the wrong things we've done."

Mackenzie and Ben were silent now as they worked, their thoughts beginning to focus on Jesus. Somehow, decorating the Jesus Tree had begun to change them on the inside.

Mackenzie opened another box and took out a glittery golden star. "I wish we had a star like this. We don't have anything for the top of our tree."

Ben stood on a chair and placed it on the highest branch. "This star is like the one which led the wise men to Baby Jesus," he said proudly. Mrs. Daniels and Mackenzie both laughed.

Well that about does it," Mrs. Daniels said as she looked the tree over. "Although, the bottom of that tree looks awfully bare. I think something is missing."

"PRESENTS!" Mackenzie and Ben shouted.

"Yes, presents," said Mrs. Daniels. "What's a birthday without any presents? There are some in the parlor." The gifts were wrapped in bright-colored paper, complete with baubles and bells and bows. Mackenzie and Ben were surprised when they realized that one of the presents was for them. "These presents are so much more than presents," Mrs. Daniels said. "They remind me of the gifts that the wise men brought to Jesus: gold, frankincense and myrrh. But more than that, they remind me of a gift God gave to me."

"God gave *you* a gift?" Ben asked.

"Yes. He gave me Jesus and He promised me a home in Heaven one day. Jesus is God's gift of love! Christmas love! Now go ahead and open your gift."

Inside the box was the most beautiful golden star for the top of their tree. "How did you know we needed one?" asked Mackenzie.

"I didn't," Mrs. Daniels replied. "But God did."

They all looked with wonder at the beautifully decorated tree and its strong lovely branches. Mrs. Daniels smiled. "Those branches are like Jesus' arms. He is always reaching out to us. When you believe in Him and make Him your King you'll find Christmas love."

The tree had seemed to transform before their eyes. It wasn't perfect, it wasn't fancy, it was just real.

"Now I will think of Jesus every time I see a Christmas tree," said Ben.

"Me too," Mackenzie smiled.

"Good, good," Mrs. Daniels said softly. "Now let's enjoy some cookies and hot cocoa."

And they shared just a little more Christmas love.

How to Put Your Faith in Jesus

God sent His only Son, Jesus, to earth in the form of a baby. That was the first Christmas. Since then Jesus died so that God could forgive us for the wrong things that we do. After his death, God raised him from the dead.

The Bible says in Romans 10:9 that if you say with your mouth that Jesus is Lord, and believe in your heart that God raised Him from the dead you will be saved.

God promises eternal life in Heaven with Him for those who believe in his only Son Jesus.